I0844065

AI and the Future of Retail

Virtual Shopping Experiences and Predictive Analytics

Table of Contents

Chapter 1. Introduction

In this illuminating Special Report, we delve into the fascinating convergence of Artificial Intelligence (AI) and the retail sector, sketching a whole new world of possibilities. As physical stores evolve and digital shopping continues to grow, unexpected changes are already underway which could revolutionize the way we purchase goods and services. From engaging virtual shopping experiences that transport you into immersive environments, to the game-changing predictive analytics that anticipate our desires even before we articulate them, this Special Report uncovers how AI is rewriting the rules of retail. This is not some far-off science fiction, but tangible transformations happening right now. So, whether you are a retailer looking to keep up with the rapidly changing industry, a tech enthusiast excited about the potential of AI applications, or simply intrigued by what the future of shopping might look like, this report will surely captivate your imagination. Embark on this fantastic journey with us, see tomorrow today, and empower yourself with the knowledge to harness this technological tidal wave.

Chapter 2. Unveiling AI: The Next Retail Revolution

Artificial Intelligence (AI) has been at the forefront of groundbreaking technological advancements in the 21st century, profoundly transforming various sectors. As the spearhead of this wave of digital disruption, it is now reshaping the retail landscape. The manifestation of AI in retail is not limited to mere speculation, but it already plays a pivotal role in redefining the parameters of consumer interaction, personalized marketing strategies, inventory management, and predictive modelling of business analytics.

2.1. AI-Based Personalized Shopping Experiences

At the heart of any successful retail business lies understanding and catering to consumer preferences. AI has elevated personalized shopping to a new stratum where consumer choices are not just merely respected but also predicted. This prediction is orchestrated through machine-learning algorithms that study historical purchase data, analyze patterns, preferences and anticipate consumer requirements.

A perfect example of AI-based personalization is product recommendations, where customers are suggested goods aligned with their interests and purchase history. It allows retailers to automate their up-sell and cross-sell strategies and significantly enhance overall sales. The interactive prompts and personalized product recommendations act as a virtual salesperson, enabling cozier, more interactive digital shopping experiences.

Besides, AI also promotes personalized marketing wherein customers are delivered targeted promotions and notifications based on shopping behavior, seasonal purchases, and offer preferences. By understanding shopper's preferences, AI helps curate a unique shopping journey for every individual, leading to higher customer satisfaction and loyalty.

2.2. Transforming In-Store Experiences

While the digital revolution has championed e-commerce, brick-and-mortar stores find their relevance in providing tactile, sensory shopping experiences that resonate with various customers. To fend off the digital disruption, physical stores are now engaging AI to improve operational efficiency, customer engagements, and enhance the shopping experience.

AI-enabled smart shelves and digital signage provide real-time inventory management, monitor stock levels, and updated pricing, thereby reducing human error while improving staff productivity. Simultaneously, AI-powered robotic assistants can assist customers in navigating the store, provide product information, and facilitate interactive shopping.

Also, keeping safety and convenience in mind, AI-enabled facial recognition technology can implement contactless transactions. The ability to collect, analyze, and store comprehensive customer behavioral data will revolutionize how brands approach, engage, and retain customers.

2.3. Predictive Analytics: The Game-Changer

A retail business thrives on data. From stock management and product demand to customer preferences and sales predictions, data helps form strategic plans and make informed decisions. AI empowers retailers by introducing predictive analytics, transforming raw, unstructured data into insightful predictions.

Predictive analytics can forecast changes in customer demand, allowing retailers to maintain an optimal inventory level, reducing the risk of stockouts or overstocking. It can also aid in adjusting pricing strategy by predicting how a particular product's pricing will influence its demand, thereby optimizing profit margins.

Furthermore, predictive analytics can forecast potential customer behavior by studying previous interactions, thus allowing retailers to engage customers proactively rather than a reactive approach. This proactive approach can significantly increase customer retention rates and facilitate more focused, effective marketing efforts.

2.4. Automating Supply Chain And Operations

AI is set to solve some of the most challenging aspects of the retail supply chain. AI-assisted automation can streamline logistics, manage inventory, track deliveries, and maintain seamless operations. Automated warehousing systems can reduce handling time, improve accuracy, and elevate the overall efficiency of distribution centers.

The use of AI in supplier selection and quality control has the potential to minimize human bias, increase transparency, and foster better supplier relationships. These applications have the power to transform the supply chain into an intelligent, self-governing system that can adapt to variations in demand, supply, and external factors.

2.5. The Future of AI in Retail

As we continue to chart the course of AI in retail, it's clear that its impact will only deepen. The blend of AI technologies, such as machine learning, natural language processing, robotics, and augmented reality, promises a future wherein 'smart retail' becomes the norm.

The convergence of AI and IoT (Internet of Things) will certainly create 'Connected Stores', which are fully-integrated, responsive, and capable of providing customized experiences to each shopper. Autonomous checkouts, AI-powered virtual shopping assistants, and personalized digital shopping interfaces will make today's innovations look elementary.

While the transformation is ongoing, it's important for retailers to understand and adapt to these changes quickly. The future belongs to those who can harness this wave of digital revolution to build more responsive, consumer-centered retail environments. The evolution from traditional shopping methods to AI-driven retail is riveting, and we are only scratching the surface of its potential.

In conclusion, AI serves as an innovative tool that retailers can employ to redefine and enhance their processes. The marriage of AI and retail may indeed herald a retail revolution, with changes that are not just innovative but transformative and beneficial for all stakeholders - businesses, employees, and customers alike. Welcome to the future of shopping, where the unprecedented interplay of AI and retail unfurls limitless possibilities.

Chapter 3. The Evolution of Shopping: From Physical to Digital and Beyond

Historically, the act of shopping has been a physiological need, driven by the necessity of trade and commerce to procure goods for sustenance and prosperity. Over time and with the evolution of society, it transformed from a mere exchange of goods into an experience, designed to cater to various human needs - emotional and physical - beyond the procurement of goods alone. It's the melding of this behavioural evolution with rapid technological advancements that usher us into the era of digital shopping we are experiencing today.

3.1. 1. The Rise of Traditional Retail

Start with the brick-and-mortar stores, which marked the first revolution in the retail sector. The first department stores in the 19th century, such as Le Bon Marché in Paris and Macy's in New York, transformed the shopping landscape. These stores designed experiences that made shopping a leisure activity, providing not only a variety of goods under one roof but also a pleasant environment to spend time in.

Over the 20th century, this model further evolved into shopping malls, strip malls, and chain stores, becoming a powerful economic force across many parts of the world. These stores leveraged various merchandising strategies, from intricate window displays to planned store layouts, enticing consumers to explore and buy more. Data analysis, though primitive compared to today's standards, played an essential role even then in understanding consumer behavior, preferences, and trends.

3.2. 2. Transition into Digital Shopping

As the century turned, the internet arrived with a new retail disruption. Initially regarded with scepticism due to reliability and security concerns, e-commerce rapidly gained momentum as technology improved. Giant marketplaces like Amazon and eBay began to dominate by offering a practically infinite selection of products at competitive prices.

In time, as internet usage soared and the digital literacy of the masses improved, the online retail sector started to blossom. Digital shopping offered consumers unparalleled convenience, allowing them to browse, compare, and purchase goods from the comfort of their homes. The growth of e-commerce was significantly catalysed by the proliferation of smartphones and increased access to high-speed internet, which made online shopping available wherever and whenever it was most convenient for the consumer.

3.3. 3. Data and Personalization in the Digital Age

Along with e-commerce came the richness of consumer data, which made it possible to glean meaningful insights on shopping behaviour. Digital shopping platforms could track a consumer's journey from the moment they entered the online store to the final sale, and this data was a goldmine.

Advanced analytics and algorithms turned this data into actionable insights, assisting retailers with personalized product suggestions based on a consumer's browsing and shopping history. Retail websites and apps began to customize content according to each consumer's unique preferences, maximizing both customer satisfaction and sales.

3.4. 4. Emergence of Multichannel Retail

Recognizing the importance of both physical and online spaces, many retailers transitioned to a multichannel strategy. This strategy incorporated a harmonized approach, where physical stores and digital platforms coexisted and cooperated to offer a seamless and consistent shopping experience.

3.5. 5. The Beyond: AI and Future Shopping Experiences

As we gaze into the future, it is clear that retail will continue to evolve, fuelled by the transformative power of Artificial Intelligence. Integration of AI into the retail experience is already underway, innovatively converging physical and digital shopping spaces.

AI solutions like chatbots and voice assistants are enhancing the online shopping experience, automating customer interactions, and providing personalized support. Virtual Reality and Augmented Reality technologies have begun to offer immersive shopping experiences, where consumers can virtually 'try on' items or envisage how a piece of furniture might look in their living room.

Predictive analytics, with AI's speed and efficiency, are becoming increasingly accurate and detailed in forecasting consumer behaviour. These systems not only anticipate product demand but can also predict emerging consumer trends, potentially taking the guesswork out of retail.

Artificial Intelligence will undoubtedly transform retail experiences even beyond what we can currently envision. Imagine smart dressing rooms in stores that suggest outfits based on the customer's previous purchases, or AI-powered personal shopping assistants that know your taste better than you do. Or consider high-tech grocery stores, where smart carts automatically add up your bill as you shop, allowing for a seamless checkout process. With AI, the possibilities are endless.

Retail, as an industry, has always thrived on innovation; AI and technology are the latest step in that evolution. The fusion of technology with the retail experience is a fascinating journey, one that we are all part of, whether as consumers, retailers, or mere observers. It's not just about shopping; it's about a shift in societal behavior and trends, a change made possible by relentless technological innovation. Shopping and retail will never be the same; as we move into this exciting, uncharted future, it will continue to morph and adapt, dictated by the ever-evolving needs of consumers and the limitless possibilities offered by technology.

Chapter 4. Taking Shopping Virtual: A Deep Dive into Augmented and Virtual Reality

Artificial Intelligence (AI) is redefining the shopping experience through innovations in augmented reality (AR) and virtual reality (VR). These technologies are creating immersive digital environments that engage shoppers not just through their senses but by surpassing existing experiences altogether.

4.1. Augmented Reality and Its Role in Retail

Augmented Reality refers to the addition of digital elements into a live view, typically through a smartphone camera or AR glasses, enhancing the real world with digital information. AR in retail offers an exciting way forward, with applications surpassing gimmicky filters into real, practical use.

Early adoption by some major retailers is further proof of AR's potential in retail. For instance, IKEA's AR app enables customers to virtually place furniture items in their homes before purchasing, giving them a realistic idea of how a product will fit within their living spaces. Similarly, online eyewear retailers have capitalized on AR, allowing customers to 'try on' glasses. These applications reduce the guesswork associated with online shopping, promoting far more confident buying decisions.

AR has also been leveraged for inside-store experiences. One example includes in-store navigation, where customers can position their smartphones in front of a shelf to see which items are in stock or on sale, quickly locate a product, or view extra information such as reviews and detailed product specs. These uses of AR are not just helping to improve the shopping experience in-store, but also making sure physical retail is an attractive option in the digital age.

4.2. Virtual Reality Changing the In-Store Experience

If AR is found at the intersection of real and digital, VR places one entirely within digitized spaces. World-leading consumer experiences now revolve around VR, with intense interest in its applicability to retail.

VR offers unique opportunities to recreate physical retail environments, which can be especially beneficial for e-commerce businesses that lack brick-and-mortar stores. A simple VR headset could transport customers to a virtual store where they can explore aisles, pick up products, and experience shopping as if they were in a physical store.

One excellent example can be seen with Alibaba's VR Mall, where shoppers can wander around shopping districts, enter stores, and pick out items. They can also interact with virtual shop assistants, gather information, and even pay for purchases — all within VR. This mode of shopping can both provide novelty and convenience for consumers, driving higher levels of engagement and experience.

Similarly, brands are using VR to create immersive brand experiences. For instance, apparel companies can create virtual fashion shows, giving the remote audience a front-row experience. Not only does this open these events up to a larger audience, but it also effectively communicates the brand story and promotes a deeper emotional connection.

4.3. Predictive Analytics, AI, AR and VR

The conjunction of AR, VR, and the power of predictive analytics presents a future shopping landscape that sounds nothing short of magical. AI is increasingly adept at discerning individual preference through browsing history and previous purchases, giving retailers unprecedented opportunities to customize user experiences.

For example, an AI might predict that a consumer who has been looking at fitness equipment could be interested in sportswear. When that consumer uses a VR shopping app, items such as sportswear could be positioned more prominently, or the virtual shopping assistant could proactively suggest related items.

Likewise, using AR for in-store shopping, customers viewing certain products might see AI-powered suggestions of complementary items. If a customer is considering a certain sofa, the AR application could also display matching side tables and lamps, uniquely curated based on their interest, style preference, and previous purchases. This combination could radically change the retail landscape, transforming how we perceive shopping.

4.4. The Future of Shopping: Opportunities and Challenges for Retailers

The integration of AI, AR, and VR in retail offers an enriching shopping experience for customers and new opportunities for retailers alike, but it also poses a significant set of challenges. Investment in such technology can be costly, and its user-friendliness and seamless integration are crucial for its success, requiring significant skill in UX design.

Privacy and security concerns loom around the collection and use of personal data. Protecting consumer information will be a significant factor in gaining consumer trust, particularly as AI begins to gather more extensive data to sharpen its predictive capabilities.

While the challenges are substantial, the opportunities they present are far greater. Retail, as we knew it, is transforming swiftly. Retailers who are proactive in adopting AR and VR technologies, while addressing potential drawbacks, may reap substantial rewards. They need to stay relevant in their customers' minds, ensuring their survival in this fast-paced, technologically driven marketplace.

In conclusion, the application of AI, AR, and VR in retail can create more personalized, immersive shopping experiences than ever before. It's not just about improving the transactional aspects of buying and selling; it's about reshaping how retailers connect with customers, pointing towards a revolutionary future in retail that we're getting a glimpse of today. As technology continues to advance, bricks-and-mortar stores won't disappear but will evolve into a new type of shopping experience, rooted in digital immersion and hyper-personalization.

Chapter 5. Predictive Analytics: Knowing the Consumer Better than They Do

In the age of e-commerce and digital marketing, retailers are now presented with the opportunity to leverage AI in understanding and predicting consumer behavior in immense detail. Recognizing that each customer is unique, with distinct characteristics, tastes, and purchase history, large corporations and SMEs alike are deploying AI-powered predictive analytics to grasp and anticipate each customer's preferences and behaviors.

5.1. Understanding Predictive Analytics

Predictive analytics revolves around the identification of future outcomes based on historical data. Leveraging statistics, data mining, machine learning, and AI, predictive analytics generates models that can anticipate, with relative accuracy, what will happen next. Traditional analytics might tell you what happened and why it happened, but predictive analytics goes further— it forecasts what could happen. It can enable retailers to target customers more accurately, recommend products they're likely to want, and make smarter business decisions.

5.2. The Mechanics of Predictive Analytics in Retail

AI-driven predictive analytics uses a combination of machine learning (ML) and big data to determine patterns. The systems comb through vast quantities of existing data to identify trends and correlations that might escape the human eye. A number of ML techniques such as regression, classification, and clustering, are employed to draw these inferences. Regression predicts continuous outcomes (like predicting sales), classification predicts categorical outcomes (like identifying if a customer would churn or not), and clustering involves grouping customers based on similarities.

Data examined typically includes past purchases, browsing history, and other customer interactions. More sophisticated models might even use external data, like weather, holidays, and events that might influence customer behavior.

5.3. Benefits of Predictive Analytics in Retail

There's no overstating the impact predictive analytics can have on the retail sector. On a surface level, it enables sophisticated targeted marketing and improves inventory management. Looking deeper, it also offers the potential for personalizing shopping experiences, promoting customer loyalty, and even predicting and managing potential risks.

Chapter 6. Predictive Analytics for Personalized Marketing

AI-powered predictive analytics is playing a pivotal role in personalization, from tailoring web, email, and app experiences, to providing personalized recommendations. With refined predictions, businesses can ensure they are suggesting the right product to the right customer at the right time.

This kind of sophisticated customization extends beyond simply suggesting similar products, predictive analytics can also determine a customer's likelihood of making a purchase and target promotions accordingly.

Chapter 7. Enhancing the Customer Experience

Personalization is not the sole avenue for enhancing the customer experience. Insight about a customer's preferences and purchase history can ensure more meaningful interactions both in-store and online, fostering a higher degree of satisfaction and loyalty. For instance, connecting in-store behavior with online data can provide a seamless and improved customer journey.

Additionally, predictive analytics can even influence store layout and design. If data suggests that a certain category of products is popular among a retailer's demographic, stores can be laid out to highlight these items.

Chapter 8. Optimizing Inventory Management

An accurate understanding of customer behaviors can lead to optimized inventory. By predicting future sales based on previous patterns, businesses are equipped to maintain optimal stock levels and avoid both overstocks and shortages, making the entire supply chain more efficient.

8.1. Potential Challenges and Risks

Despite vast potential, predictive analytics in retail is not devoid of challenges. Retailers may face issues about data quality and integration, accuracy of models, and transparency of AI algorithms.

The accuracy of predictive analytics is only as good as the data it's built on. Consequently, the quality and diversity of data play a major role in the effectiveness of predictive analytics.

Moreover, creating an appropriate model that fits the data and a specific problem is critical. Using an inadequate model or failing to consider important variables can render predictions inaccurate.

Lastly, AI algorithms can sometimes become complex "black boxes", making it difficult to understand how they are making predictions. This lack of transparency can make it challenging for businesses to fully trust the AI.

8.2. Final Thoughts

The advent of AI-powered predictive analytics is being heralded as a quantum leap for the retail sector, one that truly brings the customer front and center. By proactively understanding and anticipating customer needs, retailers can provide a personalized shopping experience that goes beyond making savvy recommendations.

However, it's essential to consider potential challenges and address them head-on to truly harness the power of predictive analytics. With careful planning and execution, retailers can benefit profoundly from this AI revolution—knowing the consumer better than they do.

Chapter 9. Personalization in Retail: How AI Makes Shopping About You

The rise of the internet and digital technology has brought a revolution in retail. No longer are consumers confined to the options available in physical stores. The digital world delivers a vast array of products and services at our fingertips, available anytime, anywhere. With the help of artificial intelligence (AI), personalization is shaping this revolution in the retail sector where shopping becomes solely about 'you.'

9.1. A New Era: Retail and AI

The use of AI in retail is not a completely new phenomenon. Retailers have long used technology to streamline their operations and enhance the customer experience. What has changed now, however, is the scale and sophistication of AI's capabilities, enabling it to deliver highly personalized shopping experiences.

AI is now able to analyze vast quantities of data, learn from this data, and make predictions or take actions that aren't specifically programmed in advance. It can identify patterns and trends that would be impossible for human analysts to find, which could be used to personalize offerings, predict demand, or optimize pricing.

9.2. Personalization: A Key Driver for Business Success

Research shows that personalization can generate significant benefits for businesses. When customers feel understood and catered to, they are more likely to convert and become loyal to the brand. Businesses implementing AI-driven personalization have experienced a rise in customer acquisition, increased customer loyalty, and enhanced overall profitability.

The potential of AI to be an enabler for personalization is immense. From providing relevant product recommendations to offering personalized customer services, AI can use its machine learning capabilities to analyze data and understand customer behavior on a granular level, providing unprecedented levels of personalization.

9.3. Personalized Product Recommendations

Tailoring product recommendations based on a consumer's buying behavior, preference, and digital behavior is one of the key applications of AI in retail. Companies like Amazon and Netflix have successfully implemented recommendation engines powered by machine learning algorithms, which analyze customers' past behavior to predict what they might want in the future. This has led to rising sales, improved customer satisfaction, and enhanced customer loyalty.

Moreover, AI could suggest products based not only on what an individual has done in the past but also in real-time, relying on contextual data such as location, occasion, and current trends.

9.4. Personalized Online Experience

AI further enhances the customer online shopping experience through chatbots, interactive screens, or digital personal shopping assistants. These AI-powered systems can answer customer queries, provide fashion advice, or help in finding a particular product. This leads to a highly personalized online shopping experience, which in turn significantly improves customer engagement and conversion rates.

Moreover, the use of cookies to monitor online browsing behavior allows AI to adapt the browsing experience in real time, showcasing the most relevant products, offers, and content to the individual user.

9.5. Predictive Personalization

Not satisfied with using just past behavior, AI can now predict future customer behavior. Predictive personalization can anticipate a customer's future needs or wants based on their existing behavior and other contextual factors. This could mean predicting a customer's size for a clothing brand, or their flavor preference for a food delivery service.

Predictive analytics can also enable retailers to manage their inventory more effectively. If a style or size is predicted to be popular, they can ensure they have enough stock to meet the demand.

9.6. Real-Time Personalization

With the development of more sophisticated AI algorithms, real-time personalization is becoming a reality. Using real-time data, AI can adapt the shopping experience in an instant. For instance, if a customer frequently purchases a brand of wine that is currently on offer, AI could immediately present this offer to the customer as they enter the online store.

By constantly adapting to each individual's actions, AI can ensure that every interaction is personalized and relevant. This could lead to a significant improvement in customer satisfaction and loyalty.

9.7. Physical Stores and AI

The impact of AI is not confined to online shopping. Physical stores are also embracing AI to enhance the shopping experience. With technologies such as face recognition and mobile location tracking, AI can personalize the in-store shopping experience.

For instance, smart signage could display personalized ads based on the customer's preferences and previous purchases. Interactive mirrors in the fitting rooms could suggest products to try, or even order the right size for the customer.

Despite the growing importance of e-commerce, physical stores still represent a significant proportion of total retail sales. By bringing AI into the stores, retailers can combine the convenience and personalization of online shopping with the tactile and social experience of physical shopping.

As AI continues to evolve and become more integrated with retail, the boundaries of personalization will keep expanding. The future of retail is likely to be one where AI, coupled with data, shapes every individual's shopping experience, ensuring that every interaction is unique, personalized, and catered to their needs and preferences. The end result? A shopping experience that is truly about 'you'.

Chapter 10. The Technology Behind the Scenes: Machine Learning in Retail

AI technologies, led by machine learning (ML) algorithms, are swiftly transforming retail operations, reshaping everything from the supply chain to the customer experience. A sophisticated form of AI, ML can learn from experience and improve its performance, opening myriad opportunities for retail.

10.1. Understanding Machine Learning and Its Types

To truly grasp the application of Machine Learning in the retail sector, it is elementary to first understand Machine Learning itself. Essentially, ML, a subset of AI, involves computer algorithms that improve automatically through experience and the use of data. Over time, these algorithms become more accurate in predicting outcomes without being specifically programmed.

ML encompasses several types but three are particularly pertinent to retail transformation: Supervised learning, Unsupervised learning, and Reinforcement learning.

In **Supervised learning**, the model is trained on a labeled dataset. By "labeled", we mean data that consists of both input parameters and an appropriate output. Some common applications of Supervised learning are regression, forecasting, and customer segmentation.

Unsupervised learning differs in that it deals with unlabeled data. The machine discovers patterns and information that wasn't known or envisaged previously. This kind of learning is best for transactional data since it can simulate user-specific recommendations.

Reinforcement learning, on the other hand, is more about interaction and adaptation. The model learns through the consequences of its actions, instead of relying on a dataset. This type of learning algorithm is used when the model needs to make a series of decisions, making it ideal for dynamic pricing and inventory management.

10.2. Machine Learning and Customer Experiences

The very heart of retail lies in customer satisfaction which hinges on understanding customer behavior and needs. Machine learning allows for deep dives into the pool of customer data, enabling better personalization and a remarkable overall customer experience.

Predictive analytics, a major application of ML, can extrapolate customer behavior to anticipate wants and needs. Machine learning can create individualized recommendations and deliver timely, relevant offers that increase sales and customer loyalty.

Virtual shopping experiences are a classic example of AI's immersion into retail. Machine learning-powered virtual dressing rooms allow customers to try clothes without physically changing, merge online and offline shopping modes, and significantly enhance shopping convenience.

10.3. Machine Learning in Supply Chain and Inventory Management

Not only does machine learning enhance the front-end customer experience, but it also optimizes back-end operations. Retailers can employ ML to streamline their supply chain and improve inventory management, leading to lower costs and increased efficiency.

Machine learning algorithms can examine historical data, analyzing patterns that allow for accurate demand forecasting. By predicting which products will be in demand, retailers can optimize their inventory levels, reducing storage costs and improving delivery times.

Moreover, ML can aid in supply chain route optimization. By analyzing factors like traffic trends, road conditions, and delivery times, machine learning algorithms can suggest the most effective delivery routes, saving time and resources expended on logistics.

10.4. The Role of Machine Learning in Pricing

Pricing is another critical retail area where machine learning can make substantial impacts. Traditional static pricing models do not consider real-time fluctuations in demand and supply. Dynamic pricing, powered by machine learning, applies flexible prices based on supply and demand.

For example, surge pricing in e-commerce is a common example of dynamic pricing. When the demand for a product increases, the prices are temporarily hiked to balance the demand-supply equation. Similarly, during times of lesser demand, prices are adjusted downwards to clear the inventory.

10.5. Challenges and Future Prospects

Despite its advantages, integrating machine learning into retail comes with challenges. The accuracy of ML algorithms depends on the quality and quantity of data inputted. Many retailers may not have access to this level of information or the capacity to process it, leading to ineffective machine learning outcomes.

Moreover, there's another crucial factor: customer privacy and data security. Retailers must walk a fine line between personalization and invasion of privacy. This requires transparent communication with customers about how their data is being used and ensuring robust security measures to protect this data.

Keeping these challenges in mind, it's clear that the future of machine learning in retail hinges on effective data management, robust security, and clear, transparent communication. With these facets in place, ML can continue to make retail smoother, more efficient, and more personalized, delivering tangible benefits to both retailers and customers.

In conclusion, the consonance of Machine Learning with retail is creating a symbiotic relationship that's reshaping the retail landscape. With forward-thinking adaptations, retailers can leverage this disruptive technology to drive enhanced profitability, improved efficiency, and unsurpassed customer experiences.

Chapter 11. Facing the Future: Ethical Considerations in AI and Retail

Technology has famously been described as a double-edged sword. On one side, Artificial Intelligence (AI) wields vast potential to drive unprecedented levels of efficiency, personalization, and convenience in the retail sector. Conversely, the widespread adoption and integration of AI also ushers in a litany of ethical considerations that retailers, regulators, and consumers must grapple with. Understanding and facing these issues head-on is crucial to ensure a future where AI in retail is not only profitable, but also just, equitable and socially beneficial.

11.1. The Ethics of Data

AI's functioning in retail is contingent on the collection, storage, and processing of enormous amounts of data. This large-scale data utilization raises a string of ethical concerns.

Firstly, there's the question of privacy. With AI being able to track and analyze each digital footprint left by consumers, what becomes of individual privacy? Should marketers have unrestricted access to consumers' online behavior? Where is the line drawn between enhanced personalization to facilitate shopping experiences from unwarranted intrusion?

Then, there's the issue of safety. In a world marred by data breaches and cyber-attacks, how do retailers guarantee that the data under their control remains secure?

Moreover, data collection practices often tend towards exclusion. The algorithms developed using this data may inadvertently favor customers who generate more data-points — typically, the tech-savvy, affluent urban demographics, leaving behind those with fewer digital traces.

Finally, data ownership too is contentious. Do consumers own their data, or do retailers? And, what about third-party advertising platforms or data analytics companies that also have access to the data? These critical questions need addressing.

11.2. AI and Employment

There are concerns AI will lead to job losses in retail. Automated checkouts, virtual assistants, and similar technologies could eliminate cashier jobs, customer service roles, and more. While proponents argue AI will also create new job categories, questions remain about the proportionality of job creation versus displacement, the nature of new jobs, and the preparedness of the current workforce to transition into new roles.

11.3. Algorithmic Decision-Making and Bias

While AI algorithms are often billed as objective, they are susceptible to biases embedded in their training data. This could lead to discriminatory practices such as dynamic pricing, where prices are adjusted based on a customer's willingness or ability to pay, or discriminatory targeting, where some demographics are systematically overlooked or targeted by the algorithms.

11.4. Algorithmic Transparency and Explainability

AI is notoriously opaque. The lack of transparency in operating mechanisms raises questions about accountability and trust—both critical to retail success. To explain the reasoning behind pricing, product suggestions, or personalized advertisements generated by AI, we need algorithmic transparency and explainability to maintain customer trust and loyalty.

11.5. The AI Divide

Finally, there's the fear of creating an AI divide. As large corporations are better-equipped to invest in expensive AI technology, they could outstrip smaller businesses, intensifying wealth and power disparities.

Confronting these issues demands solid ethical guidelines, robust regulatory frameworks, and the development of technical solutions, such as secure data storage practices, bias audit tools, and explainable AI technologies. It also involves fostering digital literacy among consumers, upskilling the workforce, and encouraging inclusive data collection practices. Only then will we achieve a promising future where AI in retail surpasses anticipated benefits while minimizing ethical issues. This dual approach, combining technical innovation with ethical steering, will ensure that we navigate the AI revolution in retail successfully and responsibly.

Chapter 12. AI in Action: Case Studies from Top Retailers

In the dynamic world of retail, where customer experience is rapidly emerging as a differentiator, industry leaders are increasingly turning to artificial intelligence (AI) to gain a competitive edge. These trailblazing companies are leveraging AI in innovative ways to revolutionize every aspect of the retail value chain. Let's explore some of these thought-provoking case studies that demonstrate AI's transformative potential in the retail sector.

12.1. Walmart: Embracing an AI-Powered Future

Underneath the familiar façade of the beloved American mega-retailer lies a vast and intricate network of AI technologies, working tirelessly to improve operational efficiency, customer experience, and overall business performance. Walmart is driving innovation in the sector through diverse AI solutions.

Walmart has extensively utilized AI in its brick-and-mortar operations. The giant's 'Intelligent Retail Lab' (IRL) store in Levittown, New York, equipped with a multitude of cameras and real-time analytics, exemplifies its AI strategy. These AI-infused innovations track inventory levels, ensure prompt replenishment, and automate mundane tasks, freeing store associates to focus on enhancing the customer experience.

Furthermore, aided by sophisticated machine learning (ML) algorithms, Walmart's 'Eden' system monitors and predicts the freshness of perishable goods spanning over 800 million items in its stores daily. This keeps customers satisfied and helps prevent food waste, demonstrating that AI can improve both business outcomes and sustainability.

12.2. Amazon: A Pioneer in AI Adoption

Undoubtedly, Amazon's innovation-driven character pushes the boundaries of what's possible in retail. Customer-centricity being Amazon's keystone principle, the company's investments in AI are aimed at offering a seamless, personalized shopping experience.

Amazon led the revolution in predictive analytics in retail with its 'anticipatory shipping' patent. The model uses customers' historical data and predictive analytics to anticipate purchases even before customers place an order. This ability to predict, pack, and ship products to a nearby location in anticipation of demand has substantially improved efficiency and speed, transforming customer expectations in the e-commerce world.

Intriguingly, Amazon's AI efforts are also physical. Amazon Go, its cashier-less store concept, merges deep learning, computer vision, and sensor fusion to allow a 'just walk out' shopping experience—eliminating queues and thus maximizing convenience.

12.3. Stitch Fix: AI in Personal Styling

A disruptor in the retail industry, Stitch Fix's business model hinges on AI and human stylists collaborating to deliver personalized fashion recommendations to customers' doorsteps.

The company's AI algorithms analyze extensive customer data, fashion trends, and feedback to curate personalized styling options. Additionally, the models optimize logistics and inventory management behind the scenes. Stitch Fix's success in combining AI and human stylists highlights AI's potential in enhancing personalization, even in the subjective domain of fashion styling.

12.4. Alibaba: Blending Physical and Digital Retail

Alibaba also illustrates the transformative potential of AI in retail. Its 'New Retail' strategy focuses on marrying the convenience of online shopping with the tactile pleasure of physical retail. AI and data analytics sit at the heart of this transformation.

One notable AI technology at Alibaba is its "FashionAI" system. The technology supports a 'smart mirror' in Alibaba's physical stores, which offers recommendations on matching outfits when customers select clothes, thereby bridging the digital-physical gap.

Alibaba's Alipay app also uses AI for risk assessment and fraud detection, ensuring secure transactions and thus fostering trust in its vast customer base.

12.5. The Home Depot: Redefining Home Improvement

The Home Depot, America's largest home improvement retailer, provides an illuminating example of how AI can ignite a digital transformation. Its use of chatbots to facilitate online customer service has proven to be a game-changer.

The company's bot, 'Zoey,' uses AI to answer customer queries about products, locate store inventory, and even help customers navigate through stores. This not only improves customer experience but also demonstrates how AI can augment human capabilities and streamline customer interaction.

These cases, representative of the wide array of AI applications in the retail sector, paint a transformative picture: companies are harnessing AI's prowess to reshape their operations, customer interactions, and decision-making processes. The adaptation and adoption of such technologies will undoubtedly become a definitive factor in choosing the market leaders of tomorrow. A profound understanding of the ongoing AI revolution should therefore be part of any forward-looking retail strategy. Stay tuned as we take a deep dive into the technologies underpinning these trends in the upcoming sections of this report.

Chapter 13. Preparing for the AI-Driven Retail Landscape: Strategies for Success

Artificial Intelligence (AI) presents a profound opportunity to augment and revolutionize the retail landscape. Retailers must adapt to this technological shift, rethinking their strategies, and meeting consumers at this intersection of technology and commerce. In this exploration, we'll delve into the meticulous strategies retailers can employ to be successful in the AI-driven retail landscape.

13.1. Understanding the Power of AI in Retail

Artificial Intelligence goes beyond the fundamental automation of processes; it offers new insights, learning from an array of data and predicting the needs of consumers with startling accuracy. Harnessing the power of AI starts with understanding just how it integrates into retail. It involves AI-driven CRM systems, Chatbots and Virtual Personal Assistants, Predictive Analytics, and Machine Learning (ML) algorithms for personalized experiences.

Personalization is no longer a luxury but an expectation on the part of the modern consumer. AI offers the possibility to personalize each customer's experience on a micro-level, presenting them with tailor-made suggestions based on their buying behavior, preferences, and demographic details.

13.2. Crafting a Comprehensive AI Strategy

Incorporating AI into your retail business needs more than casual or piecemeal integration. It requires a thorough and comprehensive AI-strategy. Start with identifying the challenges you need to solve. It could be improving customer service, optimizing the supply chain, or enhancing personalized shopping experiences. Once identified, retailers can explore using AI technologies applicable to their challenges.

Another integral part of crafting your AI strategy is assembling the right team. You'll need data scientists, AI specialists, engineers, and strategists who can design, implement, and manage AI systems. For small and medium-sized retailers, partnerships with AI service providers could be the right approach.

13.3. Scaling AI Across All Business Functions

For maximal effectiveness, retailers should aim to integrate AI across all business operations, replacing traditional methods that rely on chance and intuition. This can range from AI-driven inventory management systems that predict stocking needs based on real-time data, to using AI in HR for hiring the right staff for specific roles.

Ensure to leverage AI for customer service. AI-powered chatbots can handle customer inquiries at any time, deliver quicker responses, and as they learn, improve their communication with customers, enhancing the overall customer experience. A step further is to use sentiment analysis to understand customer emotions better and respond appropriately.

13.4. Stewarding Consumer Data Responsibility

With AI, comes the responsibility of handling vast amounts of consumer data. Retailers need to develop a robust data-governance framework to ensure that data is effectively managed, secured, and employed appropriately to respect privacy regulations. Ethical AI use teaches us that while AI improves retail operations, it should not infringe on a customer's privacy.

When customers share their data, they do so with trust that the business will guard it responsibly. Retailers need to ensure this trust isn't violated by deploying secure AI systems and applying stringent data protection protocols.

13.5. Promoting an AI-Centric Culture

Shifting towards an AI-driven retail landscape implies a significant culture change. To promote an AI-centric culture, start by educating all levels of your organization about the benefits of AI. Provide training to equip them with skills needed to effectively use AI tools. An informed employee is an empowered one.

Moreover, retailers need to demonstrate a commitment to the technology. This means not just adopting AI but advocating for its ethical use, ongoing research, and development. Only then can retailers effectively drive the adoption rates necessary to excel in an AI-dominated industry.

13.6. Adapting to an Evolving Retail Landscape

The transformative effects of AI will inevitably lead to changes in the retail landscape that are yet unknown. This necessitates continuous learning and adaptation. Retailers should keep up with AI trends, invest in relevant research and development, and be ready to pivot as the technology evolves.

In conclusion, thriving in an AI-driven retail environment involves understanding the power of AI, framing a comprehensive strategy, integrating AI across all operations, responsibly handling consumer data, promoting an AI-centric culture, and maintaining flexibility. Retailers who can do this will not just survive in this new landscape; they will flourish, creating a seamless shopping experience that breeds brand loyalty and stands out from the competition. With AI, the future of retail shines bright. The task now is to seize it.

Chapter 14. Forecast: Projecting the Future of AI in the Retail Sector

AI is on a fast track to permeating multiple sectors of our lives and the economy, and retail is no exception. This is hardly surprising considering the tremendous potential AI holds for retailers. With AI, brick-and-mortar locations can revitalize their consumer experience while online platforms can further refine and personalize their offerings. The implications are intriguing if not downright exciting. Let's explore the ways retail might evolve through the lens of AI—as both a partner and enabler of innovation.

14.1. Technological Tidal Wave: AI's Ballroom Blitz

AI's progression into retail is by no means a trickle; it's a torrent. Retailers are leveraging AI technologies like machine learning, natural language processing, computer vision, robotics and more to innovate at every level. Machine learning's predictive capabilities allow retailers to forecast consumer preferences based on past purchase patterns, online searches, and social media interactions. Robotics and computer vision help streamline in-store logistics and enhance consumer interaction. AI's potential in retail is fully reflected in IDC's forecast which stipulates that by 2022, worldwide spending on AI will reach $77.6 billion, with retail leading all other industries.

14.2. Personalized Purchasing: The AI Advantage

A future with AI promises shopper experiences tailored to personal preferences and immediate requirements. AI assists retailers in better understanding their individual customers, by analysing past purchases, browsing behaviors, and interactions with advertisements. Interactions will no longer be about mass communication but uniquely crafted messages catering to individual tastes. Big players like Amazon and Alibaba are already harnessing AI to refine their personalized recommendation engines, so it's only a matter of time before more businesses follow suit.

Also, AI-powered Chatbots are empowering retailers to offer personalized assistance to online shoppers. These bots are programmed to understand customer needs, guide them to suitable products, answer queries in real-time, and even recommend items based on context. As AI natural language processing improves, the quality of these interactions will only get better.

14.3. High-Tech Fitting Rooms and Virtual Shopping Assistants

Imagine stepping into a store and being greeted by a virtual shopping assistant who knows your taste in fashion better than you do. Your items are pre-selected, and a high-tech fitting room awaits you. The mirror inside doubles as an interactive screen, offering you alternatives, suggesting accessories, and allowing you to check out without ever leaving the room. This might seem far-fetched, but AI is rapidly bridging the gap between imagination and reality. Companies like Farfetch, an online luxury fashion retail platform, is already working on such futuristic concepts.

14.4. Smarter Inventory Management and Demand Forecasting

AI introduces robustness into supply chain systems, enabling a more efficient and dynamic inventory control. Through accurate predictive analysis, AI tools can help retailers anticipate sales trends, resulting in optimal stock levels and minimized waste. Retailers can go a step further by coupling AI with IoT (Internet of Things). By analyzing data from RFID (Radio Frequency Identification) tags and GPS, retailers can gain real-time insights into their inventory minimizing issues like stock outs and overstock.

14.5. Enhanced Security

AI isn't solely about improving sales and customer experience—security is another domain where AI has significant applications. Unauthorized access, theft, and fraud can be mitigated effectively through AI surveillance systems. By analyzing patterns and identifying unusual behavior, AI brings an extra layer of security in both, physical stores and e-commerce platforms.

14.6. The Flipside: Ethical and Privacy Concerns

Despite the enormous advantages, AI's invasion into the retail sphere is not without its challenges. As AI becomes more entwined with consumer behavior, the boundaries of privacy become increasingly blurred. Retailers can now gather unprecedented amounts of personal data—but should they? The ethical implications are vast and governments worldwide are investigating regulatory means to maintain a balance between technological advancements and individual privacy.

The clock is ticking on the future of retail. Whatever form it takes—AI is destined to play an unrivaled role. Retailers that can seize this technology, adapt to its evolving implications, and address associated challenges will steer the future of this industry. The onus lies on every stakeholder in the retail landscape to understand and harness AI conscientiously and optimally for our collective and sustainable benefit. Each tick, each tock brings a new possibility—only made possible by the momentous advent of AI.

www.ingramcontent.com/pod-product-compliance
Lightning Source LLC
Chambersburg PA
CBHW071007260726

48661CB00007B/2835